HULLABALOO-B

and 42 other songs

selected and arranged by
Barrie Carson Turner

For RST and the children of Ley Hill School, Northfield, Birmingham

Melody edition

First published 1988

Published by
MACMILLAN EDUCATION LTD.
Houndmills Basingstoke, Hampshire RG21 2XS
and London
Companies and representatives
throughout the world

Distributed to the music trade by
INTERNATIONAL MUSIC PUBLICATIONS
Southend Road
Woodford Green, Essex IG8 8HN

Printed in Hong Kong

ISBN 0–333–39904–8

Acknowledgements

We are grateful to the following publishers for permission to reproduce copyright material:

Chappell Music Ltd & International Music Publications for Cherry Pink and Apple Blossom White © 1950 Hortensia – Music, Paris, assigned 1950 Chappell & Co Inc © 1952 Chappell Music Ltd, London W1Y 3FA; Get Me to the Church on Time © 1956 Chappell & Co Inc USA, Chappell Music Ltd, London W1Y 3FA; Green Green © 1958 New Christy Music Co, Chappell Morris Ltd, London W1Y 3FA; Hey Look Me Over © 1960 Morley Music Co USA, assigned to Edwin H Morris & Co Inc, Chappell Morris Ltd, London W1Y 3FA; The Inch Worm © 1951 Frank Music Corp USA, Anglo Pic Music Ltd, London W1Y 3FA; Island in the Sun © 1956 Clara Music Pub Corp USA, Chappell Music Ltd, London W1Y 3FA; King of the Road © 1966 Tree International USA, Burlington Music Pub Co Ltd, London W1Y 3FA; The Market Song © 1981 Chappell Music Ltd, London W1Y 3FA; Robin Hood © 1944 Official Music Co Inc USA, Chappell Music Ltd, London W1Y 3FA; Who Wants to Be a Millionaire? © 1955 Chappell & Co Inc USA, Chappell Music Ltd, London W1Y 3FA.

EMI Music Publishing Ltd & International Music Publications for Any Old Iron © 1911 Herman Darewski Music Publishing Co, London WC2H OLD; Believe in Tomorrow © 1979 EMI Music Publishing Ltd, London WC2H OLD; Happiness © 1963 Moss Rose Publications Inc USA, sub-published by Moss Rose Music Ltd, London WC2H OLD; Matchstalk Men and Matchstalk Cats and Dogs © 1977 Great Northern Pub Co Ltd, sub-published by EMI Music Publishing Ltd, London WC2H OLD; Paddy McGinty's Goat © 1917 Francis Day & Hunter Ltd, London WC2H OLD; The Runaway Train © 1925 Shapiro Bernstein & Co Inc USA, sub-published by B Feldman & Co Ltd, London WC2H OLD; The Skeleton Stomp © 1980 EMI Music Publishing Ltd, London WC2H OLD; Someone Else I'd Like to Be ©1951 Peter Maurice Music Co Ltd, London WC2H OLD; Tie Me Kangaroo Down © 1960 Castle Music Pty Ltd, Australia, sub-published by Ardmore & Beechwood Ltd, London WC2H OLD.

International Music Publications for Busy Round; Garage Round © 1983 International Music Publications, Essex IG8 8HN and By and By; By the Waters of Babylon; Drill Ye Terriers; Everybody Loves Saturday Night; Freight Train; Guy Fawkes; The Helston May Song; Hullabaloo-Balay; Hush Little Baby; Jamaica Farewell; La Paloma; The Leaving Of Liverpool; Mango Walk; Oliver Cromwell; Over The Hills and Far Away; Sing Hosanna; The Spanish Guitar; This Train is Bound for Glory; Turn the Glasses Over; While Strolling Through the Park; The Work of the Weavers arranged Barrie Carson Turner © 1988 International Music Publications, Essex IG8 8HN.

Williamson Music Ltd & International Music Publications for My Favourite Things © 1959 Williamson Music Inc USA, Williamson Music Ltd, London W1Y 3FA.

How to use the chord table and fill in your chord box

Which group are you in? Look below at the instructions for your group.

Group 1

You need not use this chord table. Turn back to the song you are preparing to play and copy the chord names as printed in this book into your own chord box.

Group 2

Place one finger on the letter name of the chord you are looking for and with your other hand run a finger down the Group 2 column until you are opposite your first finger. Is the chord you are looking for made up of a single capital letter? If so, the note you need is the *first* note in column 2. If the chord has a small 'm' after it (it might also have a '7' but you needn't worry about this) you will need the note *after* the stroke. Copy this note into your chord box whenever you see the same chord letter name.

Group 3

Place one finger on the letter name of the chord you are looking for and with the other hand run a finger down the Group 3 column until you are opposite your first finger. Copy this note into your chord box whenever you see the same chord letter name.

Group 4

Place one finger on the letter name of the chord you are looking for and with your other hand run a finger down the Group 4 column until you are opposite your first finger. Is the chord you are looking for made up of a single capital letter? If so, you want the *second* note in column 4. If the chord has a small '7' after it (it might also have an 'm' but you needn't worry about this) you will need the note *before* the stroke. Copy this note into your chord box whenever you see the same chord letter name.

Chord table

Chord Letter Names	Groups			
	1 (play root)	2 (3rd)	3 (5th)	4 (7th or root)
C	C	E/E♭	G	B♭/C
D	D	F♯/F	A	C/D
E♭	E♭	G	B♭	D♭/E♭
E	E	G♯/G	B	D/E
F	F	A/A♭	C	E♭/F
G	G	B/B♭	D	F/G
A	A	C♯/C	E	G/A
B♭	B♭	D	F	A♭/B♭
B	B	D♯/D	F♯	A/B

Contents

Any Old Iron

Words and Music by CHAS. COLLINS,
E. A. SHEPPARD & FRED TERRY

Moderately

1. Just a week or two a-go my poor old Un-cle Bill, Went and kicked the buck-et and he

left me in his will. The oth-er day I popped a-round to see poor Aunt-ie Jane, She

said, 'Your Un-cle Bill has left to you a watch and chain.' I put it on

right a-cross my vest, Thought I looked a dan-dy as it dan-gled on my chest.

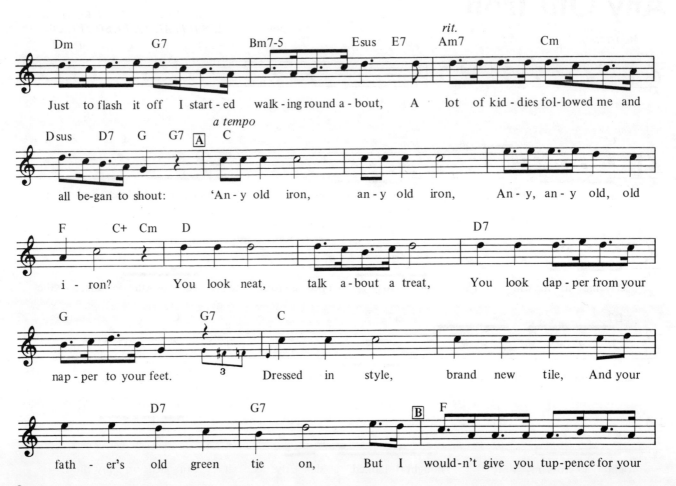

Just to flash it off I start-ed walk-ing round a-bout, A lot of kid-dies fol-lowed me and all be-gan to shout: 'An-y old iron, an-y old iron, An-y, an-y old, old i - ron? You look neat, talk a-bout a treat, You look dap-per from your nap-per to your feet. Dressed in style, brand new tile, And your fath-er's old green tie on, But I would-n't give you tup-pence for your

old watch chain, Old i - ron, old i - ron? i - ron?

2. I went to the city once and thought I'd have a spree.
   The Mayor of London, he was there, that's who I
       went to see.
   He dashed up in a canter with a carriage and a pair,
   I shouted, 'Holler boys' and threw my hat up in
       the air.
   Just then the Mayor, he began to smile.
   Saw my face and then he shouted, 'Lummy, what
       a dial!'
   Started a-Lord Mayoring and I thought that I
       should die
   When pointing to my watch and chain he hollered
       to me, 'Hi'.

   Chorus

3. Just to have a little bit of fun the other day,
   Made up in my watch and chain, I went and drew
       my pay.
   Then got out with a lot of other Colonels 'on the
       loose',
   I got full right up to here in fourp'ny 'stagger juice'.
   One of them said, 'We want a pot of ale.
   Run him to the rag-shop, and we'll bung him on
       the scale.'
   I heard the fellow say, 'What's in this bundle that
       you've got?'
   Then whisper to me kindly, 'Do you want to lose
       the lot?'

   Chorus

4. Shan't forget when I got married to Selina Brown.
   The way the people laughed at me, it made me
      feel a clown.
   I began to wonder, when their dials began to crack,
   If by mistake I'd got my Sunday trousers front to
      back.
   I wore my chain on my darby kell,
   The sun was shining on it and it made me look a
      swell.
   The organ started playing and the bells began to
      ring,
   My chain began to rattle, so the choir began to
      sing.

Chorus

Chord Box

Play from Ⓐ — Ⓑ.
Count quick 4.

C	C	C	F
D7	D7	D7	G
C	C	C ¦ D7	G

Untuned percussion

Play the rhythm of the words as indicated:

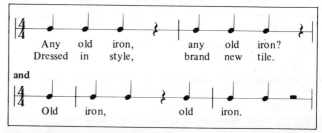

4/4	Any old iron,	any old iron?
	Dressed in style,	brand new tile.

and

| 4/4 | Old iron, | old iron. |

Play these rhythms during the chorus. Listen for
the right words.

Busy Round

Words and Music by EILEEN DIAMOND

① *Brightly*

Bus - y, bus - y, bus - y, bus - y,

② Work all the day,

③ Nev - er get a time to rest un - til you're

④ old and grey.

Accompaniment Ostinato

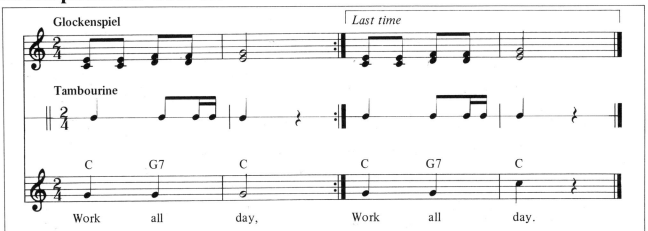

Glockenspiel

Last time

Tambourine

C G7 C C G7 C

Work all day, Work all day.

By the Waters of Babylon

Traditional

Slowly

By_____ the wa - ters, the wa - ters of Bab - y - lon.

We sat down and wept, ___ and wept ___ for thee, Zi - on.

We re - mem - ber thee, re - mem - ber thee, re - mem - ber thee, Zi - on.

Accompaniment Ostinato

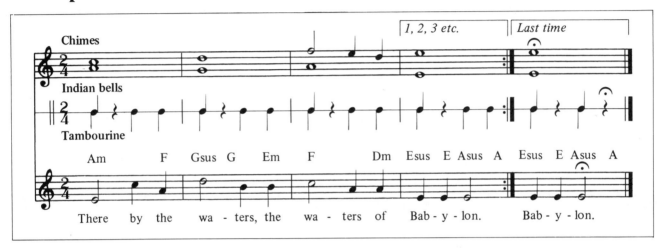

13

By and By

Traditional Spiritual

Slow blues tempo

Oh,

Chorus

by__ and by,__ By__ and by,__ I'm goin' a lay down my heav-y load, Oh,

by__ and by,__ By__ and by,__ I'm goin' a lay down my heav-y load.

1. I know my robe goin' a fit me well.___ I'm goin' a lay down my heav-y load, I

tried it on at the gates of hell. _____ I'm goin' a lay down my heav - y load. Oh,

2. My father met me at the door.
   I'm goin' a-lay down my heavy load.
   My brother he bin gone before.
   I'm goin' a-lay down my heavy load.

   Chorus

3. My children coming after me.
   I'm goin' a-lay down my heavy load.
   They're from this weary world set free.
   I'm goin' a-lay down my heavy load.

   Chorus

Chord Box

Chorus — Count 4 for each box.

F	Bb	Bb	F	Bb	F
F	Bb	Bb	F	Bb	F

15

Believe in Tomorrow

Words and Music by PETER CANWELL

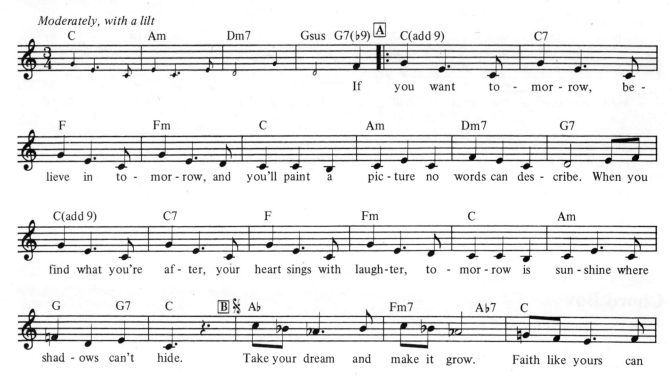

Moderately, with a lilt

If you want to - mor - row, be - lieve in to - mor - row, and you'll paint a pic - ture no words can des - cribe. When you find what you're af - ter, your heart sings with laugh - ter, to - mor - row is sun - shine where shad - ows can't hide. Take your dream and make it grow. Faith like yours can

make it so. All you long for must come true, for I be - lieve in you. So

beg, steal or bor - row, be - lieve in to - mor - row; It's there round the

cor - ner, just one dream a - way. So re - mem - ber the sec - ret: reach out for to -

mor - row, And make it hap - pen to - day.

CODA

make it _____ hap - pen to - day. _____

17

Chord Box

Play from A — B . Play boxes 1–8 only from C — D .
Count slow 3.

C	C7	F	Fm
C	Am	Dm7	G7
C	C7	F	Fm
C	Am	G7	C

Tuned/Untuned Percussion

Play from B — C . Use 1 to 4 players.

Garage Round

Words and Music by EILEEN DIAMOND

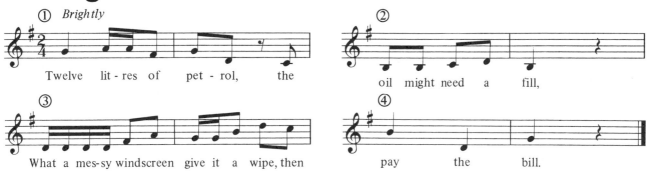

① Brightly

Twelve lit - res of pet - rol, the

② oil might need a fill,

③ What a mes-sy windscreen give it a wipe, then

④ pay the bill.

Accompaniment Ostinato

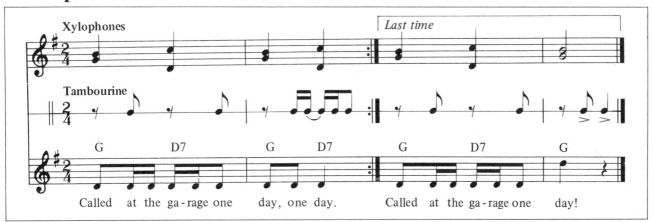

Xylophones

Last time

Tambourine

G   D7   G   D7   G   D7   G

Called at the ga-rage one day, one day.   Called at the ga-rage one day!

Everybody Loves Saturday Night

Traditional Nigerian

Lively Calypso beat

1. Ev - ery - bod - y loves Sat - ur - day night, Ev - ery - bod - y loves Sat - ur - day night, Ev - ery - bod - y, ev - ery - bod - y, Ev - ery - bod - y, Ev - ery - bod - y, Ev - ery - bod - y loves Sat - ur - day

1, 2, etc. night.

Last time night.

20

Chord Box
Play from [A] to the end of the song. Count quick 4 for each box.

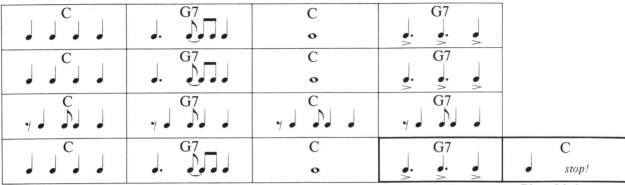

Play this bar to repeat the song.

Play this bar to finish the song.

2. **French**
Tout le monde aime
Samedi soir, *(twice)*
Tout le monde, *etc.*

3. **German**
Jedermann liebt Samstag
abend, *(twice)*
Jedermann liebt, *etc.*

4. **Italian**
Tutti vogliono il sabato sera, *(twice)*
Tutti vogliono, *etc.*

Accompaniment Ostinato

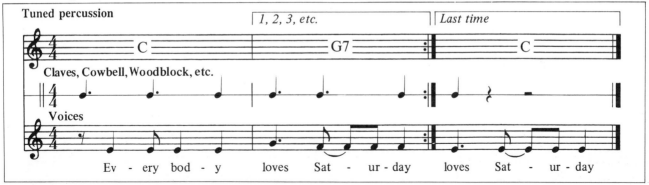

Freight Train

Traditional

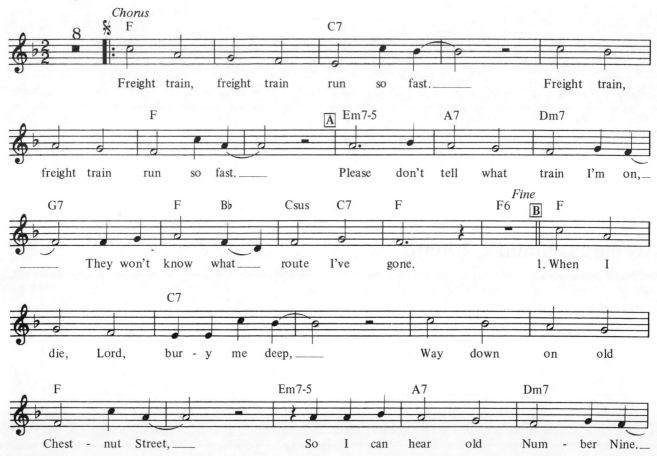

Freight train, freight train run so fast. _____ Freight train, freight train run so fast. _____ Please don't tell what train I'm on, _____ _____ They won't know what _____ route I've gone. 1. When I die, Lord, bur - y me deep, _____ Way down on old Chest - nut Street, _____ So I can hear old Num - ber Nine. _____

22

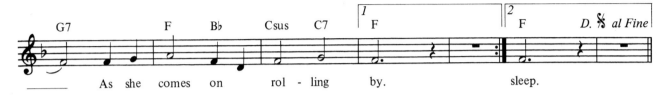

G7　　　　　F　Bb　Csus　C7 ｜1 F ｜2 F　D. 𝄋 al Fine

As she comes on rol - ling by.　　　sleep.

2. When I'm dead and in my grave,
   No more good times here I'll crave.
   Place the stones at my head and feet,
   And tell them all that I've gone to sleep.

   Chorus

Chord Box

Play from 𝄋 — A .
Count quick 2 for each box.

F	F	C7	C7
o	o	♩♩♩ ‿	o
C7	C7	F	F
o	o	♩♩♩ ‿	o

Play at the end of each chorus.

...gone.

Play four times from 𝄋 — A .

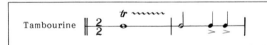

Play four times from A — B .

23

Cherry Pink and Apple Blossom White

French words by JAQUES LARUE
English words by MACK DAVID
Music by LOUIGUY

It's cher-ry pink and ap-ple blos-som white, ___ When your true lov-er comes your way.

It's cher-ry pink and ap-ple blos-som white, ___ The po-ets say.

The stor-y goes that once a cher-ry tree, ___ Be-side an ap-ple tree did grow,

And there a boy once met his bride to be, ___ Long, long a-go. The boy looked

Tuned/Untuned percussion

The following accompaniment for the verse is to be played between [A] and [B], as marked in the score. Choose which rhythms to play from the suggestions, or use your own ideas.

Notice that an extra part bar is always needed to finish off the tune.

Play a half and whole note accompaniment for the middle section of the song, between [C] and [D].

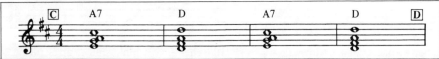

Drill Ye Terriers

Traditional American

With a heavy beat

1. Ev - ery morn - ing at sev - en o' clock There were twen - ty ter - ri - ers a - work-ing on the rock. The boss comes a - long and he says, "Keep still And come down heav - y on the cast iron drill." And

Chorus

drill, ye ter - ri - ers, drill. Drill, ye ter - ri - ers, drill. And you work all day for the sug - ar in your tea, Down be - hind the

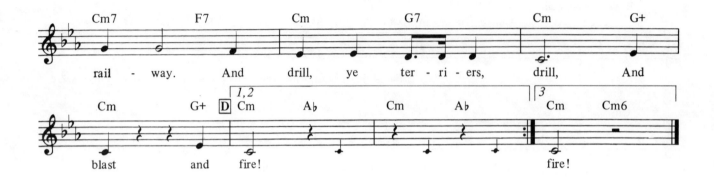

2. The new foreman's name was John McCann.
   O Lord, he was a blame mean man.
   Last week, a premature blast went off
   And a mile in the air went big Jim Goff.

   Chorus

3. When the next pay-day came around,
   Jim Goff a dollar short was found.
   When he asked what for, he got this reply,
   'You were docked for the time you were up in the sky'.

   Chorus

28

Untuned percussion

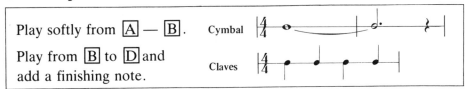

Play softly from [A] — [B].

Play from [B] to [D] and add a finishing note.

The chorus can be highlighted with this line which can either be sung or played on an instrument.

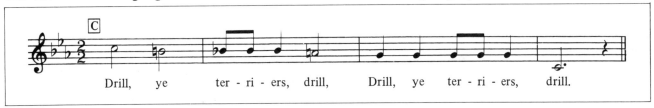

Drill, ye ter - ri - ers, drill, Drill, ye ter - ri - ers, drill.

Green, Green

Words and Music by
*BARRY McGUIRE and
RANDY SPARKS*

30

got - ta be trav - el - in' on,   A - sing - in'... on. Ev - ery-bod - y now...

2. No, there ain't nobody in this whole wide world,
   Gonna tell me how to spend my time.
   I'm just a good lovin' ramblin' man.
   Say Buddy could you spare me a dime?

   Chorus

3. I loved that man with all my heart.
   I will 'till the day I die.
   I was just a stop along his way,
   Never even said goodbye.

   Chorus

Untuned percussion

Chorus — Play the following twice. Use the words
to help you play the rhythms correctly.

4. Yeah, I don't care when the sun goes down,
   Where I lay my weary head.
   In a green, green valley or a rocky road,
   It's there I'm gonna make my bed.

   Chorus

Chord Box

Play from A — B .
Count 4 for each box.

Gm	Dm	E♭	B♭	E♭	F7	B♭
Gm	Dm	E♭	B♭	E♭	F7	B♭

Two-tone Woodblock or Cow bell

Green, green

Claves

It's green they say

Tambourine

On the far side of the hill

31

Guy Fawkes

Traditional

Brightly, quite fast

1. I sing a dole-ful tra-ged-y, Guy Fawkes, that prince of sin-is-ters, Who once blew up the House of Lords, The King and all his min-is-ters; That is, he would have blown them up, And folks would soon for-get___ him: His will was good to do the deed, That

Chorus

is if they'd ha' let___ him.___ Tow, row, row,

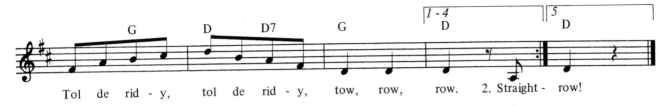

Tol de rid - y, tol de rid - y, tow, row, row. 2. Straight - row!

2. Straightway he came from Lambeth side,
   And wishes the state it was undone,
   And crossing over Vauxhall bridge,
   Came he that way into London:
   That is, he would have come that way,
   To perpetrate his guilt, sir;
   But the river was too wide to jump,
   And the bridge, it wasn't built, sir.

   Chorus

3. He sneaked into that dreary vault
   At 'witching time o'night, sir,
   Resolved to fire the powder train
   With portable gaslight, sir!
   That is, he would have used the gas,
   But solely was prevented,
   'Cause gas, you know, in James's time,
   It wasn't then invented.

   Chorus

4. Now, James, you know, was always thought
   To be a very sly fox,
   So he bid 'em search th'aforesaid vault,
   And there they found poor Guy Fawkes.
   For that he meant to blow them up,
   I think there's little doubt, sir,
   That is, I mean, provided he
   Had not ha'been found out, sir!

   Chorus

5. Now let us sing, 'Long live the King,'
   And bless his royal son, sir;
   And may he never be blown up!
   That is, if he have one, sir.
   For, if he has, he'll surely reign,
   For so predicts my song, sir;
   And if he don't, why then he won't,
   And so I can't be wrong, sir.

   Chorus

Chord Box

Chorus — Count 2 for each box.

Untuned percussion

Chorus

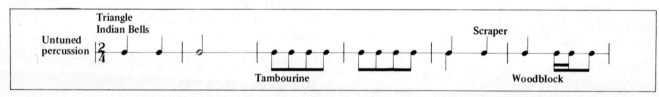

Get Me to the Church on Time

Words by ALAN J. LERNER
Music by FREDERICK LOEWE

I'm get-ting mar-ried in the morn-ing _____ Ding! Dong! The bells are gon-na chime. _____ Pull out the stop-per; Let's have a whop-per; But get me to the church on time! _____ time! _____ If I am danc-ing, _____ Roll up the floor! _____

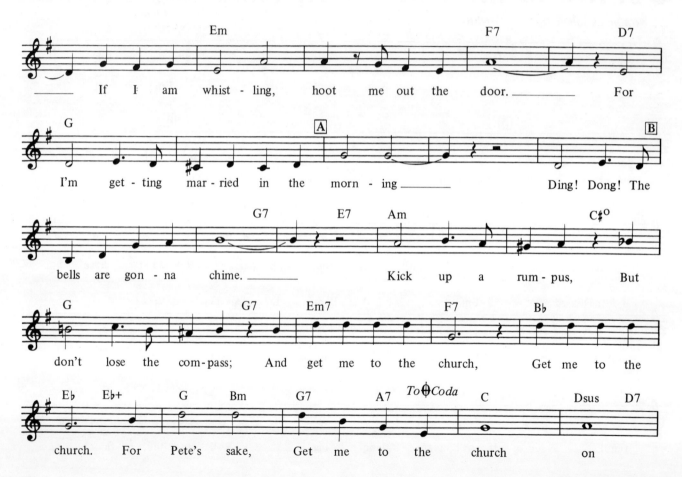

36

The following chord pattern occurs six times, always beginning on: 'I'm getting married in the morning'.

Chord Boxes Count very quick 4 (or slow 2).

G	G	G	G
o	o	♩ ♩	o
G	G	G	G │
o	o	♩ ♩	♩ │ *stop!*

Only play the following if plenty of instruments and players are available. Use very resonant chimes, but stop them sounding at the chord changes.

Em7	F7	B♭	E♭ │
o	o	o	♩ │ *stop!*

... And get me to the   church.   Get me to the   church.

Untuned percussion

The words beneath these notes show you when to play. Everyone also plays on the last chord of the song.

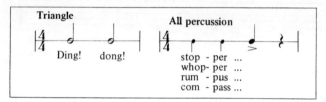

Tuned percussion

Play from A — B and from C — D. (Note that the second A — B, because of the repeat, finishes during the bar marked 𝄋.)

Happiness

Words and Music by BILL ANDERSON

Hap - pi - ness, ___ hap - pi - ness, ___ the great - est gift ___ that I pos - sess, ___ I thank the Lord ___ that I've been blessed ___ with more than my share of hap - pi - ness. ___ *Verse* 1. To

me this world is a won - der - ful place, I'm the luck - i - est hu - man in the
2. Hap - pi - ness is a field ___ of grain, Turn - ing its face to the

hu - man race, ___ I've got no sil - ver and I've got no gold, But
fal - ling rain, ___ I see it in the sun - shine, breathe it in the air,

more than my share of hap - pi - ness. ____   hap - pi - ness. ____

Chord Boxes

F group
Chorus — count 4 for each box.

F	Bb	C7	F
F	Bb	C7	F

G group
Verse — count 4 for each box.

G	C	D7	G
G	C	D7	G
G	C	D7	G
G	C	D7	G

The Helston May Song

Traditional

1. Ro - bin Hood and Lit - tle John, They_ both are gone_ to the fair, O; We will to the mer-ry green-wood To_ see what they_ do_ there, O. For to chase the_ buck and doe, To_ chase the buck _ and _ doe, O, For to chase the_ buck and doe, With_ Hal - an - tow_ sing_ mer - ry, O. mer - ry, O.

2. We were up as soon as day
   To fetch the summer home, O;
   Summer and the sweet May, O,
   For summer is a-come, O.
   Winter is a-gone, O,
   And summer is a-come, O,
   Winter cold is now gone, O,
   With Hal-an-tow sing merry, O.

3. Good Saint George shall be our song;
   Saint George he was a knight, O;
   Of all the kings in Christendom,
   King George he is the right, O.
   In each land that e'er we go
   Sing Hal-an-tow and George, O,
   In each land that e'er we go,
   Sing Hal-an-tow and George, O.

Chord Box

Play from A — B . Count 2 for each box.

D	Bm	D	A7	D	G	A7	D
D	Bm	D	A7	D	G	A7	D

Untuned percussion
Play from B — C .

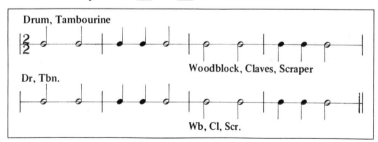

43

Hey, Look Me Over

Words by CAROLYN LEIGH
Music by CY COLEMAN

Hey, look me o - ver, lend me an ear;_____ fresh out of clo - ver, mort-gaged up to here._____ But don't pass the plate, folks, don't pass the cup;_____ I fig - ure when-ev- er you're down and out, the on - ly way is up. And I'll be up like a rose - bud, high on the vine;_____

Don't thumb your nose, bud, take a tip from mine. I'm a lit-tle bit short of the el-bow room, but let me get me some, And look out, world, here I come.__

The lower notes are an optional harmony line.
Sing them or play them on instruments.

Chord Box

Play from A — B and C — D.
Count quick 2 for each box.

G	G	B	B
E7	E7	Am	Am

Hullabaloo-Balay

Traditional

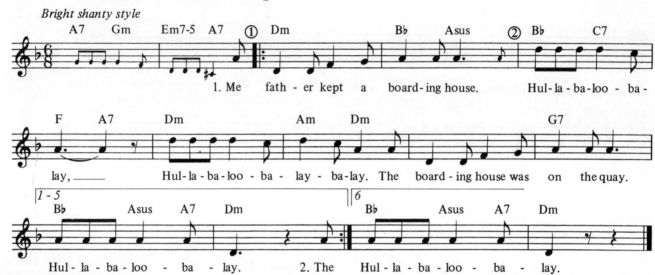

Bright shanty style

1. Me fath - er kept a board - ing house. Hul - la - ba - loo - ba -

lay, ____ Hul - la - ba - loo - ba - lay - ba-lay. The board - ing house was on the quay.

Hul - la - ba - loo - ba - lay. 2. The Hul - la - ba - loo - ba - lay.

2. The boarding house was on the quay.
Hullabaloo-balay,
Hullabaloo-balay-balay.
The lodgers nearly all at sea,
Hullabaloo-balay.

3. A flash young man called Shallow Brown,
He followed me mam all round the town.

4. Me father said, 'Young man, me boy',
To which he quickly made reply.

5. Next day when dad was in The Crown,
Me mam ran off with Shallow Brown.

6. Me father slowly pined away,
For mam came back the following day.

Accompaniment Ostinato

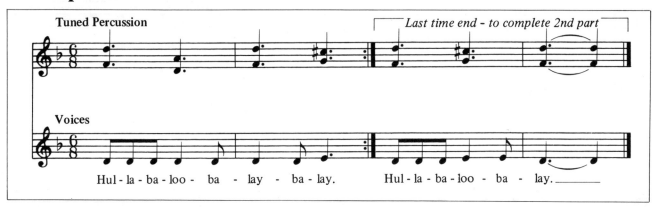

Hush Little Baby

Traditional

1. Hush lit - tle ba - by, don't say a word, Mam-ma's gon-na buy you a mock-ing bird. And if that mock-ing bird won't sing, Mam- ma's gon - na buy you a dia - mond ring. 2. And ba - by in town.

2. And if that diamond ring is brass,
Mamma's gonna buy you a looking-glass.
And if that looking-glass gets broke,
Mamma's gonna buy you a billy goat.

3. And if that billy goat won't pull,
Mamma's gonna buy you a cart and bull.
And if that cart and bull turn over,
Mamma's gonna buy you a dog called Rover.

4. And if that dog called Rover won't bark,
Mamma's gonna buy you a Noah's ark.
And if that Noah's ark goes down,
You'll still be the sweetest little baby in town.

Chord Box

Play from ⒶⒷ — ⒷⒷ . Count 4 for each box.

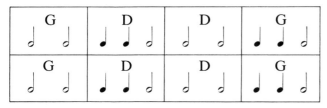

Untuned percussion

Play the rhythm of the words as follows (each subject occurs twice). All the rhythms are the same as:

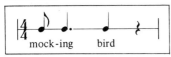

except:

Everybody plays:

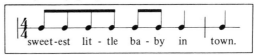

Instruments

mocking bird	—	scraper
diamond ring	—	triangle
looking-glass	—	jingles
billy goat	—	drum
cart and bull	—	tambourine
dog called Rover	—	woodblock
Noah's ark	—	claves

The Inch Worm

Words and Music by FRANK LOESSER

Inch-worm, inch worm, mea-sur-ing the ma-ri-golds, You and your a - rith-me - tic, you'll prob-ab - ly go far. Inch - worm, inch - worm, mea-sur - ing the ma - ri - golds, Seems to me you'd stop and see how beau-ti - ful they are. Two and two are four, Four and four are eight, Eight and eight are six - teen, Six - teen and six -

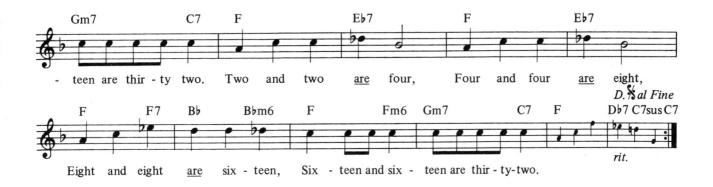

- teen are thir - ty two. Two and two are four, Four and four are eight,

Eight and eight are six - teen, Six - teen and six - teen are thir - ty-two.

D. % al Fine

rit.

Chord Box

Play the following chords, when you hear the words beneath. The chord pattern occurs six times when the song is sung through with the repeat. Count slow 3 for each box.

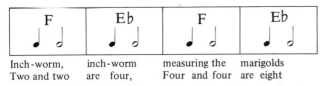

F	Eb	F	Eb
Inch-worm,	inch-worm	measuring the	marigolds
Two and two	are four,	Four and four	are eight

Island in the Sun

Words and Music by
HARRY BELAFONTE and LORD BURGESS

52

2. When morning breaks the heaven on high
   I lift my heavy load to the sky,
   Sun comes down with a burning glow,
   Mingles my sweat with the earth below.

   Chorus

3. I see woman on bended knee
   Cutting cane for her family,
   I see man at the water's side
   Casting nets at the surging tide.

   Chorus

4. I hope the day will never come
   That I can't wake to the sound of drum,
   Never let me miss carnival
   With calypso songs philosophical.

   Chorus

Chord Box

Begin at A and play the chord sequence twice for each time through the song.

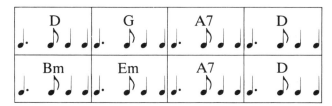

Untuned percussion

Jamaica Farewell

Traditional

1. Down a-way__ where they sing all day__ And the sun shines dai-ly on the mountain top.__ I took a trip on a sail-ing ship__ And when I reached Jam-ai-ca I made a stop.__ But I'm sad to say__ I'm on my way__ Won't be back for man-y a day__ My heart is sad__ my eyes are turn-ing a-round__ I had to leave a lit-tle girl in King-ston town.__ King-ston town.__

2. Sounds of laughter everywhere,
   See the dancing girls swaying to and fro;
   I must declare that my heart is there,
   'Though I've been from Maine to Mexico.

   Chorus

Chord Box

Tuned percussion
Count 4 for each box.

D	G	A7	D
D	G	A7	D

3. Down at the market you can hear ladies
   Cry out, while on their heads they bear
   Ackie, rice, salt fish on ice,
   And the rum is fine any time of year.

   Chorus

Untuned percussion

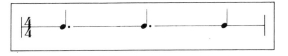

La Paloma

Spanish

Latin American style

The night _____ is _____ warm, I hear the cic - a - das trill. _____ And

soon _____ in the woods the night - ing - ales will sing. _____ The

2 ____ *1* Soon we shall meet and dance the hab - an - er - a, _____

Thril - ling to touch, I'll ten - der - ly hold her near - er. _____ La Pal - o - ma they

56

call her,___ But her eyes are like dark wine;___ And their depths I shall see_ some day, Be -

cause now I know she's mine._____ La Pal - o - ma they mine._____

Tuned/Untuned percussion

The accompaniment for this song is divided into three parts, A, B and C. Follow the words and you will see when to play.

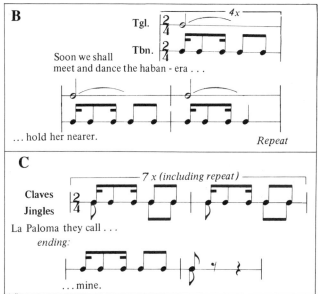

King of the Road

Words and Music by ROGER MILLER

Moderately slow

1. Trail-er___ for sale or rent;___ Rooms___ to let___ fif-ty cents;___ No phone,___ no pool, no pets;___ I ain't got no ci-gar-ettes.___ Ah, but two hours___ of push-ing broom buys a eight___ by twelve___ four-bit room___ I'm a man of

means   by   no means   King__ of the   Road.   Road.   I know

ev - er - y   en - gin - eer   on   ev - er - y   train.__   All   of   the   child - ren   and

all   of their names__   And   ev - er - y   hand - out   in   ev - er - y town.__   And

ev - ery lock that ain't locked when   no-one's a - round.__ I sing   *Dal Segno for v. 2*   Road.

(Second time through) to Coda

2. Third box car, midnight train;
   Destination Bangor, Maine.
   Old worn-out suit and shoes;
   I don't pay no union dues.
   I smoke old stogies I have found,
   Short but not too big around.
   I'm a man of means by no means
   King of the Road.

Chord Box

Play from ⒜— ⒝. Count 4 for each box.

Bb	Eb	F7	Bb
Bb	Eb	F7	F7
Bb	Eb	F7	Bb
Bb	Eb	F7	Bb

Untuned percussion

Play the rhythm of the words as indicated:

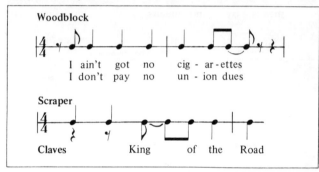

Notice that in the Chord Box the first, third and fourth lines are the same, and only the final chord of the second line is different.

The Leaving of Liverpool

Traditional

Slow, relaxed tempo

1. Fare thee well the Prin - ces land - ing stage, Riv - er

Mer - sey, fare thee well; For I'm bound for Cal - i - for - ni- a, a place that I know right

Chorus

well. So fare thee well my own true love, when I re-turn u - ni - ted we shall

Tuned Percussion:

be; It's not the leav - ing of Liv - er-pool that grieves me, but my dar-ling when I think of

thee. 2. Yes, I'm

2. Yes, I'm bound for California* by way of stormy
   Cape Horn,
   But you know I'll write to you a letter, my love,
   when I'm homeward bound.

   Chorus

3. I have shipped on a Yankee clipper ship, Davy
      Crockett is her name,
   And her captain's name, it is Burgess, and they
      say she's a floating shame.

   Chorus

4. It's me second trip with Burgess and I reckon to
      know him well.
   If a man is a sailor then he'll be alright, but if not,
      why he's sure in hell.

   Chorus

*Cal-if-or-ny-ay

Chord Box

Play from [A]— [B]. Don't play the boxes that are crossed out (but still continue counting so you know when to play again). Count slow 4 for each box.

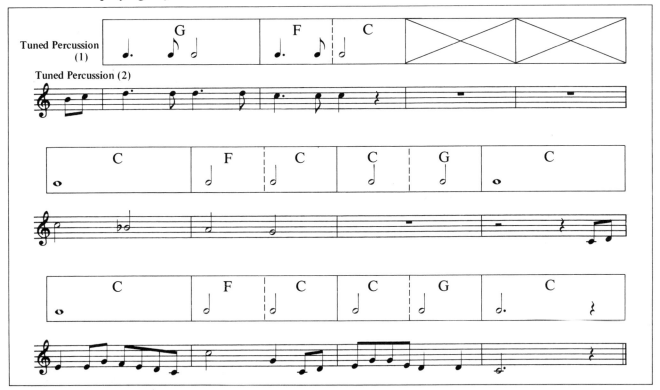

The Market Song

Words and Music by
EILEEN DIAMOND

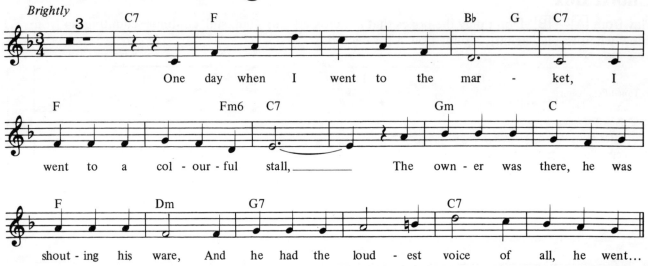

One day when I went to the mar - ket, I went to a col - our - ful stall, _____ The own - er was there, he was shout - ing his ware, And he had the loud - est voice of all, he went...

Untuned percussion

Chorus — each pair of percussionists plays with a group of singers.

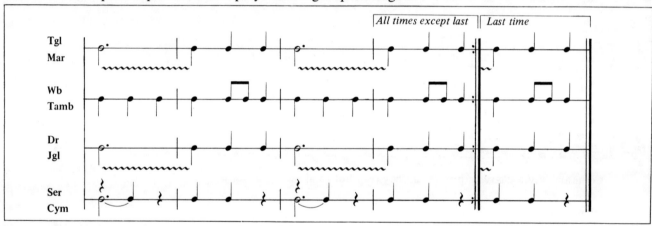

Mango Walk

Traditional

My broth-er did-a tell me that you go man-go walk, You

go man-go walk, you go man-go walk, My broth-er did-a tell me that you go man-go walk. And

steal all the num-ber e - le - ven. 1. Now tell me, Joe, do tell me for true, Do

tell me for true, do tell me, That you don't go to no man-go walk. And

steal all the num-ber e - lev - en. Now lev - en. My lev - en.

67

The following melodies can be played or sung at the same time as the verse. They can be played one by one or all together. Try singing the verse through on its own before adding the extra melodies.

1 & 2. La-la-la, *etc.*

1. Tell me, Joe, do tell me true, That
2. Tell you Sue, I tell you true, That

1. Joe do tell me for true, do tell me for true, do tell me, That
2. Sue I tell you for true, I tell you for true, I tell you, That

you)
I } don't go And steal all the number e - lev - en.

you)
I } don't go man - go walk And steal all the number e - lev - en.

68

Chord Boxes

Count 4 for each box.

Chorus

F	F	C7	F
o	♪♪ ♪♪	♪♪ ♪♪	♩ ♩ −
F	F	C7	F
o	♪♪ ♪♪	♪♪ ♪♪	♩ ♩ −

Verse

C7	F	C7	F
♩♩♩♩	♪♩ ♪♩	♪♩ ♪♩	♩ ♩ −
C7	F	C7	F
♩♩♩♩	♪♪ ♪♪	♪♪ ♪♩♩	♩ ♩ −

Untuned percussion

Play throughout, with a pause between chorus and verse.

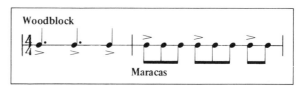

Oliver Cromwell

Traditional

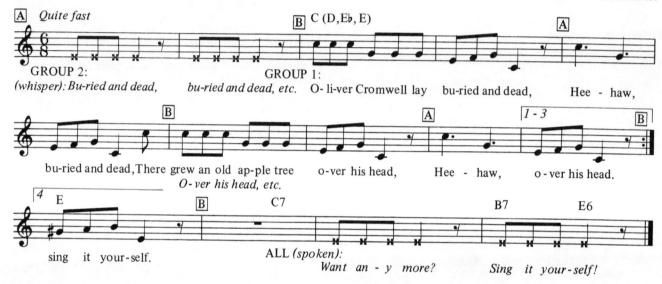

GROUP 2:
(whisper): *Bu-ried and dead,*   *bu-ried and dead, etc.*

GROUP 1:
O- li-ver Cromwell lay   bu-ried and dead,   Hee - haw,

bu-ried and dead, There grew an old ap-ple tree   o-ver his head,   Hee - haw,   o-ver his head.
O- ver his head, etc.

sing it your-self.   ALL *(spoken):*
Want an - y more?   *Sing it your-self!*

2. The apples were ripe and *ready to fall,*
Hee-haw, ready to fall,
There came an old woman to *gather them all,*
Hee-haw, gather them all.

3. Oliver rose and he *gave her a drop,*
Hee-haw, gave her a drop,
Which made the old woman go *hippety-hop,*
Hee-haw, hippety-hop.

4. The saddle and bridle they *lie on the shelf,*
Hee-haw, lie on the shelf,
If you want any more you can *sing it yourself,*
Hee-haw, sing it yourself.

Spoken:
Want any more?
Sing it yourself!

Tuned percussion

Play from [A] — [B] (three times each verse).

Verse 1 — C
2 — D
3 — E♭
4 — E

Untuned percussion

Play at the end of each line:

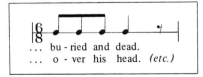

... bu - ried and dead.
... o - ver his head. *(etc.)*

Over the Hills and Far Away

Traditional

1. Hark! now the drums beat up a gain, For all true sold-iers, gen-tle-men, Then let us 'list, and march, I say, O-ver the hills and far-a-way. O'er the hills and o'er the main to Flan-ders, Port-u-gal and Spain, Queen Ann com-mands, and we'll o-bey, O-ver the hills and far-a-way. 2. All far-a-way.

2. All gentlemen that have a mind
   To serve the Queen that's good and kind,
   Come 'list and enter into pay
   Then over the hills and far away.

   Chorus

3. Here's forty shillings on the drum
   For those that volunteers do come,
   With shirts, and clothes and present pay,
   When over the hills and far away.

   Chorus

4. For if we go 'tis one to ten
   But we'll return all gentlemen,
   All gentlemen as well as they,
   When over the hills and far away.

   Chorus

5. What though our friends our absence mourn
   We with all honour shall return,
   And then we'll sing both night and day
   Over the hills and far away.

   Chorus

Tuned percussion

Play from B — C (*3 times*).

Untuned percussion

Play from A — B (8 times).

My Favourite Things

Words by OSCAR HAMMERSTEIN II
Music by RICHARD RODGERS

1. Rain-drops on ros - es and whis - kers on kit - tens, Bright cop - per ket - tles and warm wool - en mit - tens, Brown pa - per pack - ag - es tied up with strings, These are a few of my fav - our - ite things.

3. Girls in white dres - ses with blue sa - tin sash - es, Snow-flakes that stay on my nose and eye -

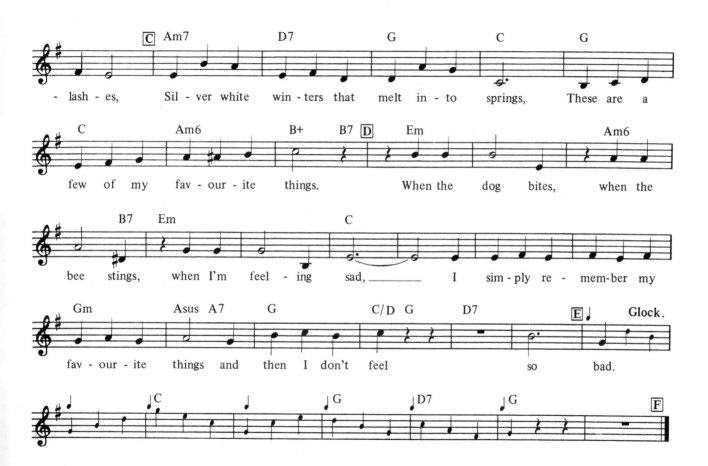

-lash - es,   Sil - ver white   win - ters that   melt in - to   springs,   These are a   few   of   my   fav - our - ite   things.   When the   dog   bites,   when the   bee   stings,   when I'm   feel - ing   sad, _____   I   sim - ply re - mem-ber my   fav - our - ite   things   and   then   I   don't   feel   so   bad.   Glock.

75

2. Cream coloured ponies and crisp apple strudels,
   Doorbells and sleighbells and schnitzel with
      noodles,
   Wild geese that fly with the moon on their wings,
   These are a few of my favourite things.

Chord Boxes

Play from A — B. (Don't forget the repeat but count the two-bar introduction first.)

Em	Em	Em	Em
C	C	C	C
Am	D7	G	C
G	C	Am	B7

Play from C — D.

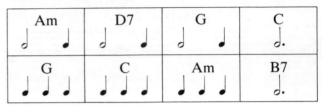

Play from E — F.

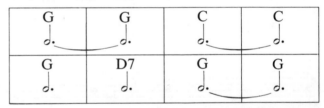

Untuned percussion

Play once at the beginning of each bar, for the first four bars and always with the following phrase:

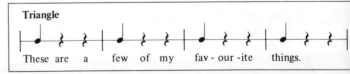

Triangle

These are a few of my fav-our-ite things.

Play also on the first beat of each of the last eight bars.

Matchstalk Men and Matchstalk Cats and Dogs

Words and Music by MICHAEL COLEMAN & BRIAN BURKE

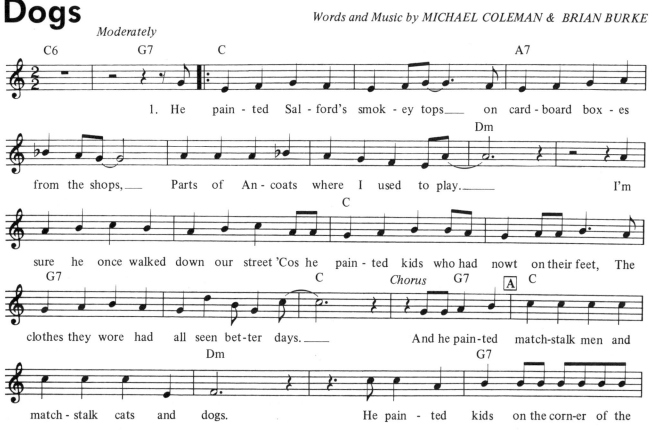

1. He pain-ted Sal-ford's smok-ey tops__ on card-board box-es from the shops,__ Parts of An-coats where I used to play.__ I'm sure he once walked down our street 'Cos he pain-ted kids who had nowt on their feet, The clothes they wore had all seen bet-ter days.__ And he pain-ted match-stalk men and match-stalk cats and dogs. He pain-ted kids on the corn-er of the

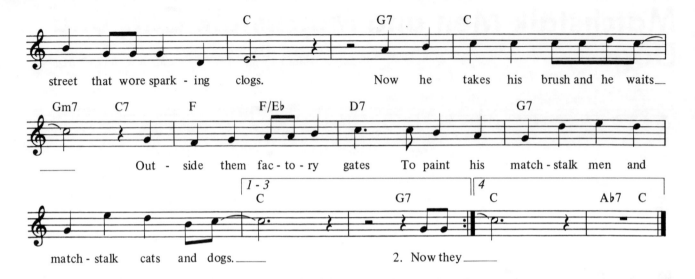

street that wore spark-ing clogs. Now he takes his brush and he waits_ Out - side them fac-to-ry gates To paint his match-stalk men and match-stalk cats and dogs._ 2. Now they_

2. Now they said his works of art were dull,
   'No room, old lad, the walls are full',
   But Lowry didn't care much anyway.
   They said, he just paints cats and dogs
   And matchstalk men in boots and clogs,
   And Lowry said, 'That's just the way they'll stay'.

   Chorus

3. Now canvas and brushes were wearing thin
   When London started calling him
   To come on down and wear the old flat cap.

They said, 'Tell us all about your ways,
And all about them Salford days.
Is it true you're just an ordinary chap?'

Chorus

4. Now Lowrys hang on every wall,
   Beside the greatest of them all.
   Even the Mona Lisa takes a bow.
   This tired old man with hair like snow
   Told northern folk, 'It's time to go',
   The fever came and the good Lord mopped his brow.

   Chorus

C o	C o	Dm o	Dm o
G7 o	G7 ♩ ♩	C o	✕
✕	✕	✕	✕
G7 o	G7 ♩ ♩	C o	✕

Chord Box

Play from A. Don't play the boxes which are crossed out (but continue counting so you know when to play again).

Count quick 4 for each box.

Untuned percussion

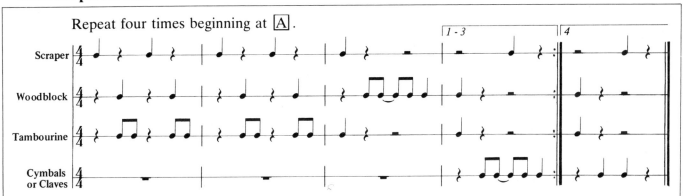

Robin Hood

Words and Music by CARL SIGMAN

Rob - in Hood, Rob - in Hood, Rid - ing through the glen, Rob - in Hood, Rob - in Hood, With his band of men, Feared by the bad, Loved by the good, Rob - in Hood, ____ Rob - in Hood, ____ Rob - in Hood, ____

1. He called the great - est arch - ers to a

tav - ern on the green, They vowed to help the peo - ple of the King. _____

They hand - led all the trou - ble on the Eng - lish count - ry scene, And

still found plen - ty of time to sing. _____ way. _____

2. He came to Sherwood Forest with a feather in his cap,
A fighter never looking for a fight;
His bow was always ready and he kept his arrows sharp,
He used them fighting for what was right.

Chorus

3. With Alan Dale and Little John, they had a roguish look,
They did the deeds that others wouldn't dare;
Recaptured all the money that the evil sheriff took,
And rescued many a lady fair.

Chorus

4. To cheating and corruption he would never, never
     yield,
     And danger was his breakfast every day;
     The cobbler in the hamlet and the farmer in the
     field
     Were always helping him get away.

   Chorus

5. He rode up to the palace and was cheered by
     every one,
     His Lady Marian threw him down a rose;
     The King of England knighted him the Earl of
     Huntingdon,
     And that's the way that the legend goes.

   Chorus

Untuned percussion
Play from B — C.

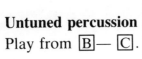

Chord Box

Play from A — B. Count 2 for each box.

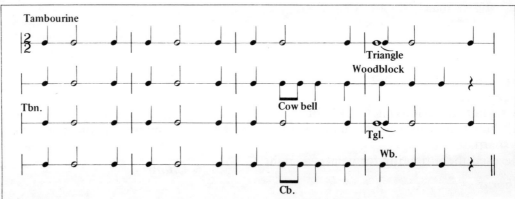

82

Paddy McGinty's Goat

Words and Music by R. P. WESTON,
BERT LEE and THE TWO BOBS

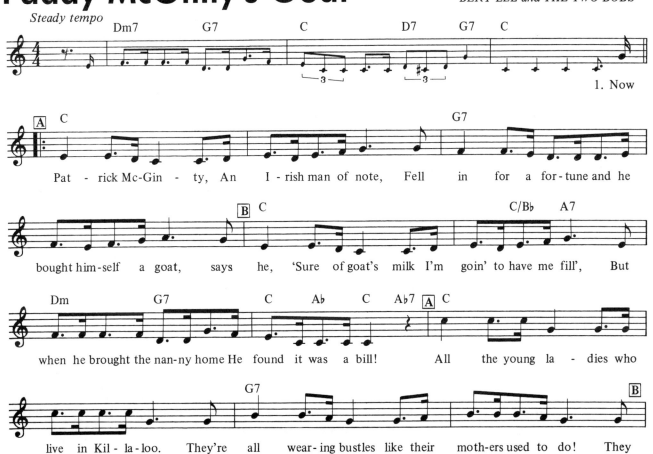

1. Now Pat - rick Mc-Gin - ty, An I - rish man of note, Fell in for a for - tune and he bought him-self a goat, says he, 'Sure of goat's milk I'm goin' to have me fill', But when he brought the nan-ny home He found it was a bill! All the young la - dies who live in Kil - la - loo. They're all wear-ing bustles like their moth-ers used to do! They

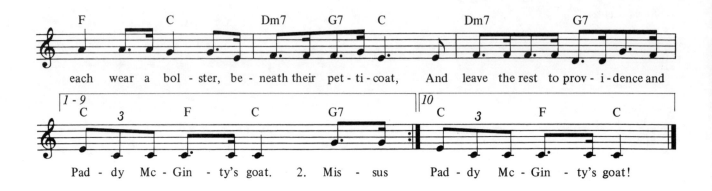

each wear a bol - ster, be - neath their pet - ti - coat, And leave the rest to prov - i - dence and

Pad - dy Mc - Gin - ty's goat. 2. Mis - sus Pad - dy Mc - Gin - ty's goat!

2. Missis Burke to her daughter said, 'Listen Mary Jane,
   Who was the man you were cuddling in the lane?
   He'd long wiry whiskers a-hanging from his chin.'
   'Twas only Pat McGinty's goat, she answered with a grin.
   She went away from the village in disgrace,
   She came back with powder and paint upon her face.
   She'd rings on her fingers, she wore a sable coat,
   You bet your life she didn't get those from Paddy McGinty's Goat.

3. Now Norah McCarthy the knot was goin' to tie,
   She washed out her trousseau and hung it out to dry,
   Along came the goat and he saw the bits of white;
   And chewed up all her falderals, upon her wedding night.
   'Oh, turn out the light quick,' she shouted out to Pat,
   'For though I'm your bride, sure I'm not worth looking at.
   I had two of everything, I told you when I wrote,
   But now I've one of nothing all through Paddy McGinty's goat.'

4. Mickey Riley he went to the races t'other day,
   He won twenty dollars and shouted, 'Hip-hoo-ray!'
   He held up the note shouting, 'Look at what I've
       got!'
   The goat came up and grabbed at it and swallowed
       up the lot.
   'He's eaten me bank note', says Mickey with the
       hump.
   They went for the doctor and they got a stomach
       pump.
   They pumped and they pumped for the twenty
       dollar note,
   But all they got was ninepence out of Paddy
       McGinty's goat.

5. Now old Paddy's goat had a wondrous appetite,
   And one day for breakfast he had some dynamite,
   A big box of matches he swallowed all serene,
   Then out he went and swallowed up a quart of
       paraffin.*
   He sat by the fireside, he didn't give a hang,
   He swallowed a spark and exploded with a bang.
   So if you go to heaven you can bet a dollar note
   That the angel with the whiskers on is Paddy
       McGinty's goat!

*para-*feen*

Chord Box

Play A — B. Count 4 for each box.

Untuned percussion

Play A — B.

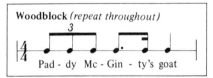

Sing Hosanna!

Traditional

Lively

1. Give me joy in my heart, keep me prais- ing, ____ Give me joy in my heart, I pray; Give me joy in my heart, keep me prais- ing, ____ Keep me prais- ing 'til the break of day. Sing Ho-san - na! Sing Ho-san - na! Sing Ho-san-na to the King of Kings! Sing Ho-san - na! Sing Ho-san - na! Sing Ho-san-na to the King! 2. Give me King!

2. Give me peace in my heart, keep me resting, *etc.*

   Chorus

3. Give me love in my heart, keep me serving, *etc.*

   Chorus

4. Give me joy in my heart, keep me praising, etc.

   Chorus

Untuned percussion

Play this bar all the way through the chorus:

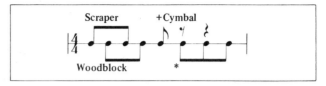

Add a 'finishing off' note after the last bar:

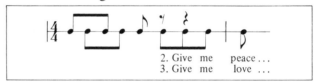

*When you can play this part easily, add variety by changing ♩♩♩ to ♩♩♩ on every second bar.

The Skeleton Stomp

Words and Music by SUE STEVENS

Stealthily, but not too slow

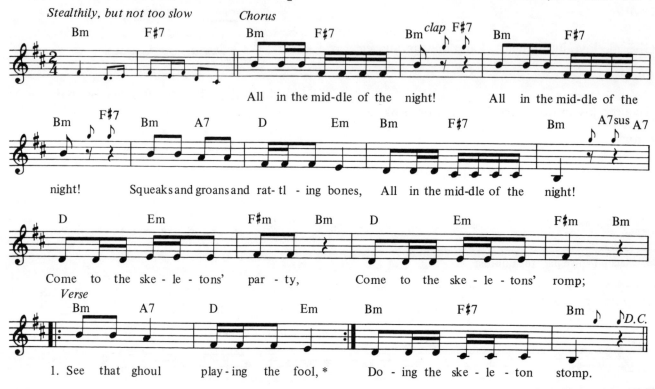

All in the mid-dle of the night! All in the mid-dle of the night! Squeaks and groans and rat- tl - ing bones, All in the mid-dle of the night! Come to the ske - le - tons' par - ty, Come to the ske - le - tons' romp;

1. See that ghoul play - ing the fool, * Do - ing the ske - le - ton stomp.

* Repeat previous verses in reverse order

2. See that cat in a pink top hat,

3. See that elf enjoying himself,

4. See that frog jiggle and jog,

5. See that toad from down the road,

6. See that ghost munching toast,

7. See that spider full of cider,

8. See that snake shimmy and shake,

9. See that witch from out of the ditch.

Tuned/Untuned percussion

This Train

Traditional

Not too fast

1. This train is bound for glor - y, this train._____ This train is bound for glor - y, this train._____ This train is bound for glor - y, Don't take none but the right-eous and ho - ly. This train is bound for glor - y, this train._____ this train. *This train!* 5. This train don't take no li - ars, this train._____

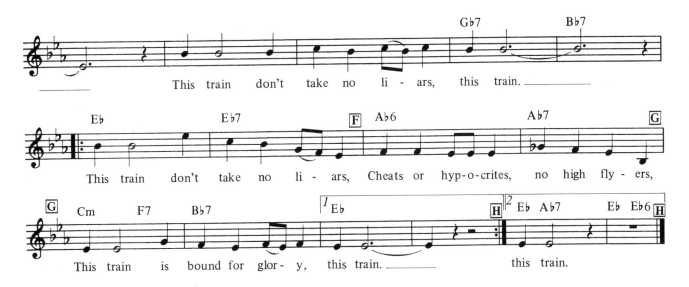

2. This train don't carry no gamblers, this train,
This train don't carry no gamblers, this train,
This train don't carry no gamblers,
No hypocrites, no midnight ramblers,
This train is bound for glory, this train.

3. This train is built for speed now, this train, *etc*
Fastest train you ever did see, now,
This train is bound for glory, this train.

4. This train don't carry no rustlers, this train, *etc*
Side street walkers, two-bit hustlers,
This train is bound for glory, this train.

5. This train don't take no liars, this train, *etc*
Cheats or hypocrites, no high flyers
This train is bound for glory, this train.

Untuned percussion

Repeat this bar between A — B, C — D, E — F and G — H.

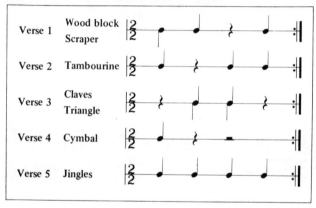

Verse 1	Wood block / Scraper	
Verse 2	Tambourine	
Verse 3	Claves / Triangle	
Verse 4	Cymbal	
Verse 5	Jingles	

Tuned percussion

Play from B — C and F — G.

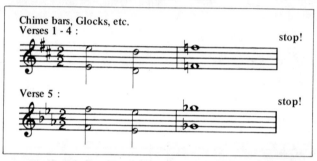

Chime bars, Glocks, etc.
Verses 1 - 4 :   stop!

Verse 5 :   stop!

The percussion parts for this song are *accumulative,* that is a new part is added for each verse until in verse 5 all the instruments are playing.

The Spanish Guitar

Traditional

Bright waltz

1. When I was a stu-dent at Ca-diz____ I played on the Span-ish guit - ar, ching, ching! I used to make love to the la-dies,____ I think of them still from a - far, ching, ching!

Chorus

Ring, ching ching, Ring ching ching, Ring out the bells, Oh, ring out the bells, Oh, ring out the bells, Ring ching ching, Ring ching ching, Ring out the bells, As I play on my Span - ish guit - ar, ching, ching!

2. I was - ar, ching, ching!

2. I was four years a student at Cadiz,
   Where nothing my pleasure could mar, ching, ching!
   There many a beautiful maid is,
   Oh I strummed and I twanged my guitar, ching,
     ching!

   Chorus

3. Oh I sang serenadiz at Cadiz,
   Till I got an attack of catarrh, ching, ching!
   Though no more could I serenadise,
   Still I played on my Spanish guitar, ching ching!

   Chorus

4. When at last the train took me from Cadiz,
   The ladies all cried round the car, ching, ching!
   Oh it grieved me to part from those ladies,
   But I carried away my guitar, ching, ching!

   Chorus

5. I'm no longer a student at Cadiz,
   But I play on the Spanish guitar, ching, ching!
   And still I am fond of the ladies,
   Though now I'm a happy papa, ching, ching!

   Chorus

Tuned/Untuned percussion

95

Tie Me Kangaroo Down

Words and Music by ROLF HARRIS

Narrator *(speaking over the introduction):* There's an old Australian stockman lying dying. And he gets himself up on to one elbow, and he turns to his mates who are gathered round him, and he says:

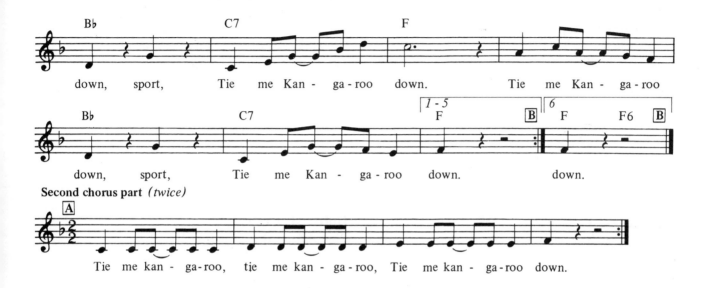

down,　　sport,　　Tie　me　Kan - ga - roo　down.　　　　Tie　me　Kan - ga - roo

down,　　sport,　　Tie　me　Kan - ga - roo　down.　　　　down.

Second chorus part *(twice)*

Tie　me　kan - ga - roo,　tie　me　kan - ga - roo,　Tie　me　kan - ga - roo　down.

2. Keep me cockatoo cool, Curl,
   Keep me cockatoo cool.
   Don't go acting the fool, Curl,
   Just keep me cockatoo cool.
   Altogether now!

   Chorus

3. Play your didgeridoo, Blue,
   Play your didgeridoo.
   Keep playing 'til I shoot through, Blue,
   Play your didgeridoo.
   Altogether now!

   Chorus

4. Take me koala back, Jack,
   Take me koala back.
   He lives somewhere out on the track, Mac,
   So take me koala back.
   Altogether now!

   Chorus

5. Mind me platypus duck, Bill,
   Mind me platypus duck.
   Don't let him go running amok, Bill,
   Mind me platypus duck.
   Altogether now!

   Chorus

6. Tan me hide when I'm dead, Fred,
   Tan me hide when I'm dead.
   So we tanned his hide when he died, Clyde,
   (*Spoken*) And that's it hanging on the shed.
   Altogether now!

   Chorus

Chord Box

Count quick 4 for each box. Play from A — B.

F	Bb	C7	F
F	Bb	C7	F

Untuned percussion

Play during the chorus only.

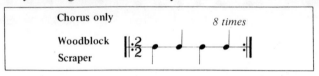

Second chorus part Sing (or play) twice.

Tie me kan - ga - roo, tie me kan - ga - roo, Tie me kan - ga - roo down.

98

Someone Else I'd Like to Be

Original Words and Music by TOM SUTTON
New Words Adaptation by BILL TURNER
& STAN BOWSHER

I were not up - on the stage some-one else I'd like to be, If I were not up - on the stage a

TAX-I DRI-VER me, You'd hear me all day long, a - sing-ing out this song:

Someone Else'd Like to Be

Policeman

1 1. TAXI DRIVER

Driv - ing tax - is, driv - ing tax - is, Honk, honk, honk, pip, pip,

2 2. WINDOW CLEANER

Clean - ing win-dows, clean - ing win-dows, Run-ning up steps all day,

Teacher

3 3. BARROW BOY

Ripe ban-an - as, ripe ban-an - as, Ap - ples a pound and pears,

Businessman

4 4. CLIPPIE

In - side on - ly, in - side on - ly, No more room on top,

Doctor

5 5. AUCTIONEER

What am I bid? What am I bid? Go - ing, go - ing, gone,

6. COALMAN

Coal - man, coal - man, large lumps for sale,

100

101

ALL: Some-one else we'd like to be, If we were not up - on the stage.

2. … a Window Cleaner me…
3. … a Barrow Boy I'd be…
4. … a Clippie I would be…
5. … an Auctioneer me …
6. … a Coalman I would be…

While Strolling Through the Park

Words and Music by
ED HALEY

With a lilt

1. I was stroll-ing through the park one day, In the mer-ry month of May, I was tak-en by sur-prise by a pair of rog-uish eyes, In a mo-ment my poor heart was stole a-way. A smile was all she gave to me.

me-di-ate-ly raised my hat, And fi-nal-ly she made re-ply, Yes, I nev-er shall for-get that love-ly af-ter-noon, I met her at the foun-tain in the park. Of

course we were as hap-py as we could be. 2. I im-

3. I was stroll - ing through the park one day,

In the mer - ry month of May, I was tak - en by sur - prise by a

pair of rog - uish eyes, In a mo - ment my poor heart was stole a - way. It hap-pened to - day!

Chord Boxes

Play from A — B. Count slow 4 for each box.

Bb	Eb		C7	F	
♩ ♩	♩	*stop!*	♩ ♩	♩	*stop!*
Bb	Eb		F7	Bb	
♩ ♩	♩	*stop!*	♩ ♩	♩	*stop!*

Play from C — D. Count slow 4 for each box.

C	F		D7	G	
♩ ♩	♩	*stop!*	♩ ♩	♩	*stop!*
C	F		G7	C	
♩ ♩	♩	*stop!*	♩ ♩	♩	*stop!*

Untuned percussion

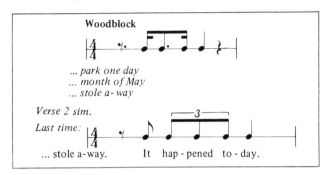

Woodblock

... park one day
... month of May
... stole a-way

Verse 2 sim.

Last time:

... stole a-way.   It   hap - pened   to - day.

Tuned percussion

Play as indicated by the small notes in the score. If you can't manage the small notes in the second bar, just play the big notes.

105

Turn the Glasses Over

Traditional

I've been to Haar - lem, I've been to Do - ver, I've trav - elled this wide world all o - ver, O - ver, o - ver, three times o - ver, Drink all the bran-dy wine and turn the glass-es o - ver. Sail - ing east, sail - ing west, Sail - ing o - ver the o - cean. Oh, you'd bet - ter watch out when the boat be - gins to rock Or you'll lose your girl in the o - cean.

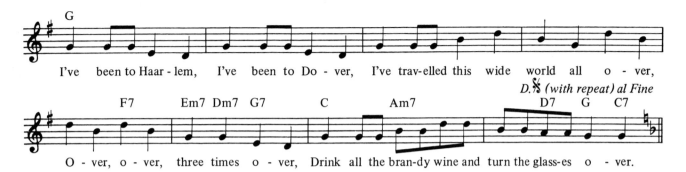

G

I've been to Haar-lem, I've been to Do-ver, I've trav-elled this wide world all o - ver,

D.% (with repeat) al Fine

F7   Em7 Dm7 G7   C   Am7   D7 G C7

O - ver, o - ver, three times o - ver, Drink all the bran-dy wine and turn the glass-es o - ver.

Chord Box

Play between $ and *Fine*.
Count slow 4 for each box.

F	F	F	C7
o	o	o	o
F	F	F	C7 F
o	o		

Tuned/Untuned percussion

Play from $ to A .

Chimes or Glocks

Cymbal

Triangle

Wood block

The Runaway Train

Words by ROBERT E. MASSEY
Music by CARSON ROBISON

2. The engineer said the train must halt,
   And she blew, (*she blew*).
   The engineer said the train must halt,
   And she blew, (*she blew*).
   The engineer said the train must halt,
   He said it was all the fireman's fault,
   And she blew, blew, blew, blew, blew.

3. The fireman said he rang the bell,
   And she blew, (*she blew*).*etc.*
   The fireman said he rang the bell,
   And she blew, (*she blew*).
   The fireman said he rang the bell,
   The engineer said, "You did like 'fun'",
   And she blew, blew, blew, blew, blew.

4. The porter got an awful fright,
   And she blew, (*she blew*) *etc.*
   The porter got an awful fright,
   He got so scared that he turned white,
   And she blew, blew, blew, blew, blew.

5. A mule was standing in the way,
   And she blew, (*she blew*) *etc.*
   A mule was standing in the way,
   And all they found was just his bray,
   And she blew, blew, blew, blew, blew.

6. A drummer sat in the parlour car,
   And she blew, (*she blew*) *etc.*
   A drummer sat in the parlour car,
   And he nearly swallowed a fat cigar,
   And she blew, blew, blew, blew, blew.

7. The conductor said there'd be a wreck,
   And she blew, (*she blew*) *etc.*
   The conductor said there'd be a wreck,
   And he felt the chills run up his neck,
   And she blew, blew, blew, blew, blew.

8. The runaway train went over the hill,
   And she blew, (*she blew*) *etc.*
   The runaway train went over the hill,
   And the last we heard she was going still,
   And she blew, blew, blew, blew, blew.

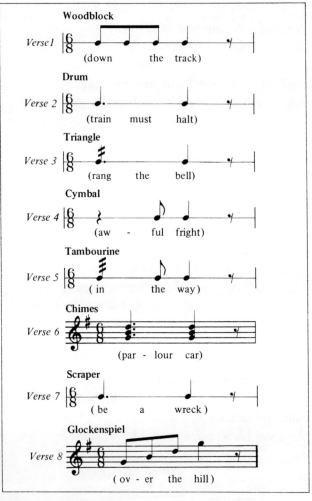

Tuned/Untuned percussion

With each repetition of *she blew* chimes, glocks, recorders (or tin whistles), or any other pitched instrument play the following notes (or any other):

(she   blew)

Who Wants to Be a Millionaire?

Words and Music by
COLE PORTER

Slow · **Moderate speed**

HE: Who has an itch to be fil - thy rich?___

SHE: Who gives a hoot for a load of loot?___

HE: Who longs to live a life of per-fect ease?___ SHE: And be swamped by

ne - ces - sar - y lux - ur - ries.___ HE: Who wants to be a mil - lion-

- aire? SHE: I don't. HE: Have flash - y flunk - eys ev - ery - where?

℁ Chorus With a bounce

SHE: I don't. HE: Who wants the both-er of a coun-try es-tate? SHE: A

coun-try es-tate? Is some-thing I'd hate! HE: Who wants to

wal-low in cham-pagne? SHE: I don't. HE: Who wants a su-per-son-ic

plane? SHE: I don't. HE: Who wants a mar-ble swim-ming pool too?

Both:
SHE: I don't, and I don't 'cause all I want is you.

Fine *al Fine*

112

Chord Box

Play from A. Don't play the boxes crossed out (but continue to count so you know when to play again). Count a quick 4 for each box.

Bb	Bb	Bb	Bb	Bb	Bb	F7	F7
F7	F7	F7	F7	F7	F7	Bb	Bb
Bb	Bb	Bb	Bb				
					F7	Bb	Bb

(... all I want is   you.)

Untuned percussion

Woodblock accompanies 'I don't' with:

(except for the last time when both parties are singing).

Untuned percussion accompanies 'Who wants' with:

For the *chorus* boys sing 'he' and girls 'she'. On the repeat they reverse the roles.

113

The Work of the Weavers

Traditional Scottish

1. We're all met to-geth-er here, to sit and to crack, With our glass-es in our hands and our work up-on our back. And there's not a trade a-mong them all can eith-er mend nor mak' if it was-na' for the work of the wea - vers.

Chorus

If it was-na' for the wea - vers what would they do? We would-na' have cloth made of our wool. We would-na' have a coat,

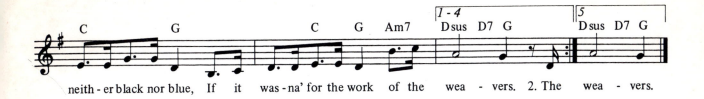

neith-er black nor blue, If it was-na' for the work of the wea - vers. 2. The wea - vers.

2. The hireman chiels, they mock us and crack aye
   aboot's.
   They say that we are thin-faced; bleached like
   cloots;
   But yet for a' their mockery they canna do wi' oot's.
   No! They canna want the work of the weavers.

3. There's our wrights and our slaters and glaziers
   and a',
   Our doctors and our ministers and them that live
   by law;
   And our friends in South America, though them
   we never saw,
   But we know they wear the work of the weavers.

4. There's our sailors and our soldiers, we know
   they're a' bold,
   But if they hadna clothes, faith, they couldna' live
   for cauld;
   The high and the low, the rich and the poor, a'
   body young and auld –
   They winna want the work of the weavers.

5. There's folk that's independent of other tradesmen's
   work.
   The women need no barbers and dykers need no
   clerk:
   But none of them can do without a coat or a shirt,
   No! They canna want the work of the weavers.

Chord Box

Play from A — B . Count 4 for each box.

Untuned percussion

If it was-n't for the work of the wea - vers.